The • Life Cycle • Series

The Life Cycle of a
BIRD

Bobbie Kalman & Kathryn Smithyman

Crabtree Publishing Company

www.crabtreebooks.com

The Life Cycle Series
A Bobbie Kalman Book

Dedicated by Heather Fitzpatrick
For my husband, Rick Nesbitt, who taught me to fly

Editor-in-Chief
Bobbie Kalman

Writing team
Bobbie Kalman
Kathryn Smithyman

Editors
Amanda Bishop
Niki Walker

Cover design
Kymberley McKee Murphy

Computer design
Margaret Amy Reiach

Production coordinator
Heather Fitzpatrick

Photo researcher
Heather Fitzpatrick

Consultant
Patricia Loesche, Ph.D., Animal
Behavior Program, Department
of Psychology, University of
Washington

Photographs
Frank S. Balthis: pages 18, 25 (top), 29 (inset)
Wolfgang Kaehler: page 9
James Kamstra: pages 11 (right), 23 (bottom right), 24
Robert McCaw: pages 19 (top left and right), 23 (bottom left)
Diane Payton Majumdar: page 17 (top)
Allen Blake Sheldon: page 19 (bottom left and right)
Tom Stack and Associates:
    Tom & Therisa Stack: page 25 (bottom right);
    Greg Vaughn: page 28
Other images by Adobe Image Library, Digital Stock,
and Digital Vision

Illustrations
Barbara Bedell: back cover, egg border, pages 4, 5 (left and right),
    6, 8, 9 (right), 10 (top), 11 (left), 22, 27
Patrick Ching: page 10 (bottom)
Cori Marvin: page 9 (left)
Margaret Amy Reiach: series logo, front cover, title page, page 24
Bonna Rouse: pages 5 (top), 7, 11 (right), 12-13 (center), 14, 21, 30-31
Doug Swinamer: page 5 (bottom)
Tiffany Wybouw: pages 12 (left), 13 (right)

Crabtree Publishing Company

www.crabtreebooks.com   1-800-387-7650

Cataloging in Publication Data
Kalman, Bobbie
    The life cycle of a bird / Bobbie Kalman & Kathryn Smithyman.
    p. cm. -- (The life cycle)
    Includes index.
    Describes how birds develop from eggs to adults, explains differences between bird
    species, and tells why some birds are endangered and what individuals can do to help
    protect them.
    ISBN 0-7787-0654-0 (RLB)   ISBN 0-7787-0684-2 (pbk.)
    1. Birds--Life cycles--Juvenile literature. [1. Birds. 2. Endangered species.] I. Smithyman,
    Kathryn. II. Title.
    QL676.2 .K3484 2002
    598--dc21   2001037210
                                                                 CIP

**Published in
the United States**
PMB 16A
350 Fifth Ave.
Suite 3308
New York, NY
10118

**Published
in Canada**
616 Welland Ave.
St. Catharines, Ontario
Canada
L2M 5V6

**Published in the
United Kingdom**
White Cross Mills
High Town
Lancaster, LA1 4XS
United Kingdom

**Published
in Australia**
386 Mt. Alexander Rd.
Ascot Vale (Melbourne)
VIC 3032

Contents

4   What is a bird?

6   What is a life cycle?

8   All kinds of eggs

10   Cosy and warm

12   Inside the egg

14   Ready to go

16   Help me, Momma!

18   Almost an adult

20   Making the long journey

22   Choose me!

24   Building a home

26   Disappearing homes

28   Helping birds in danger

30   For the birds

32   Glossary and Index

What is a bird?

Birds are **warm-blooded** animals. You are also warm-blooded. The inside of a bird's body stays the same temperature in cold and warm weather. Birds are the only animals with feathers. Feathers keep birds warm and protect their bodies.

The toucan uses its bill to reach berries, fruit, and seeds in its rainforest home.

This male northern cardinal has feet for perching in trees and a bill that is suited to eating seeds.

There are 9000 different **species**, or kinds, of birds. Birds come in many shapes, sizes, and colors. Even though they look different, all birds have the same body parts—a beak, two wings, two legs, and feathers.

*The crab plover is a type of **shorebird**. It lives and feeds along ocean shores.*

*There are several **flightless** birds, including the emu, the ostrich, and the cassowary, above. They have strong legs for running.*

Raptors are birds that catch prey with their feet, as this hawk is doing.

Penguins are flightless birds. Their tiny wings work as flippers. Penguins swim underwater to catch fish and squid.

The flamingo has long legs for wading through water. It bends its long neck to scoop food from the mud at the bottom of a lake or lagoon.

Both dinosaur and bird!

Scientists believe that birds **evolved**, or came from, dinosaurs. This picture shows a fossil of an **Archaeopteryx**, one of the first animals known to have feathers. This bird ancestor lived 150 million years ago.

Archaeopteryx

What is a life cycle?

The great white egret lives in marshy areas throughout the southern parts of the world.

A **life cycle** is made up of all the stages that an animal goes through from the time it begins its life until it is fully grown. Each life cycle includes the same stages—being born or hatching, growing, and changing into an adult that can make babies of its own. With each new baby, the life cycle starts again.

A bird's life span

An animal's **life span** is different from its life cycle. A life span is the length of time an animal is alive. It ends when the animal dies. A life cycle is repeated again and again. The cycle is arranged as a circle on the opposite page to show that it does not end.

A bird's life cycle

A bird's life cycle begins with an **egg**. Baby birds **hatch** to get out of their eggs. The **hatchlings** grow into **fledglings**, which are **immature** birds. When they have finished growing, they become **mature**, or adult, birds. Some birds **migrate**, or travel long distances, as part of their life cycles. Other birds spend their whole lives in one area.

adult

egg

hatchling

fledgling

7

All kinds of eggs

common loon

robin

pheasant

osprey

hummingbird

Every spring, male and female birds **mate** in order to make babies. After they mate, the females lay eggs. A baby bird starts to grow inside each egg. The developing baby is called an **embryo**.

Why lay an egg?

Many animal mothers carry babies inside their bodies until the babies are ready to be born, but birds cannot. A mother bird would be too heavy to fly if she had a baby inside her. Instead, she lays eggs. The hard shells protect the embryos so they can grow outside her body until they are ready to hatch.

Big eggs, little eggs

Bird eggs come in a variety of sizes. Large birds usually lay big eggs, whereas small birds lay little eggs. For example, a hummingbird's egg is the size of a pea, but an ostrich's egg is the size of a cantaloupe.

snowy owl

murre

tern

cassowary

Don't fall off the ledge!

Most bird eggs are oval, the same shape as that of a chicken egg. Some sea birds, such as murres, lay eggs that are pointed at one end. These birds live on rocky ledges above the ocean. If their eggs are bumped, the pointed ends make them roll in a small circle instead of rolling off the ledge.

These thick-billed murres lay their eggs on rocky island ledges in the Arctic.

Hidden eggs

Common loons, ospreys, and many other birds lay **camouflaged** eggs. The shells of camouflaged eggs have colors or patterns that blend in with their nests. The eggs above are camouflaged. **Predators** find it difficult to spot them in the wild. Predators are animals, including other birds, that eat eggs and baby birds.

Ostriches are the largest birds, and they lay the biggest eggs.

Cosy and warm

A bird embryo can grow only if the egg is **incubated**, or kept warm. Birds **brood**, or sit on, their eggs to keep them warm. Some bird parents take turns brooding so that each can leave the nest to feed. The females of other bird species do not leave the nest at all. Their mates bring them food.

Brightly colored male birds, such as this wood duck, do not help raise the eggs. Colors attract predators, so these males stay away from the nests. Their female mates cover the eggs with grass or leaves when they leave their nests to find food.

The male honeycreeper, above, feeds his mate while she is brooding. Honeycreepers live in Hawaii and are very rare. Only three of these birds were found in the year 2000.

All at once

Most birds lay more than one egg. Birds that live on the ground wait until they have laid all their eggs before they begin brooding them. They do this so that all the eggs will hatch at the same time.

First ones first

Birds that nest in trees, such as owls, brood each egg as it is laid. The first owlet that hatches is larger and stronger than the others in the nest. Sometimes it eats all the food, causing the smaller owlets to starve.

Caring fathers

The male emperor penguin, left, incubates an egg by resting it on his feet, off the cold ground. He has a flap of skin called a **brood pouch**, which covers the egg and keeps it warm. A male blue-footed booby, right, helps his mate brood eggs. Both male and female boobies use their webbed feet to incubate eggs.

Inside the egg

A chicken develops inside an egg in the same way that all other birds do. While the mother hen patiently broods the egg, the chick inside grows and changes quickly.

On the first day, the embryo starts out as a tiny dot, but every few hours, new body parts grow. The chick grows a **backbone** and then a head. By the end of the first week, its heart is fully formed and starts pumping blood.

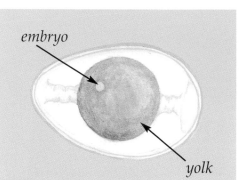

embryo

yolk

*Day 1: The tiny embryo is attached to the egg by a cord. The embryo sits on top of the **yolk**, which is its food.*

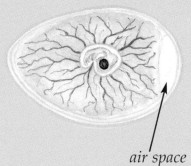

air space

Day 7: Blood vessels attached to the yolk carry food to the embryo. While its heart is forming, the chick starts to grow legs, wings, and a beak.

By the twelfth day, the embryo has a head, a neck, wings, and claws on its feet. Its beak is hardening, and its skin has small bumps, called **feather germs**, from which feathers start to grow. The chick is still small enough to move around inside the shell.

By day 21, the chick has grown too big for its shell. It hatches by cracking the shell with its sharp **egg tooth**. It pushes itself out of the shell using its strong neck muscles.

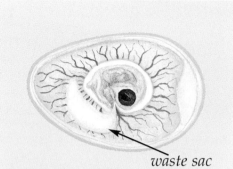

waste sac

Day 12: The embryo has two large black eyes. Eyelids grow over the eyes to protect them. Feathers grow, covering the chick's body.

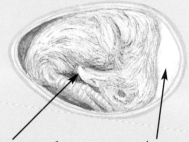

egg tooth   air space

*Day 20: The chick has used up most of the yolk. Its body is fully formed and has feathers. On this day, the chick pushes its beak into the **air space** and breathes air with its lungs for the first time. It will hatch the next day.*

Ready to go

Chickens, geese, ducks, pheasants, and gulls are **precocial** birds. They live on the ground. Precocial babies can stand, walk, or swim within a few hours of hatching. If these baby birds were helpless when they hatched, they would be easy targets for predators. The babies need to  keep warm while they move around. They have thick fluffy feathers, called **down**.

See and do

Precocial babies leave the nest soon after they hatch. They are able to move quickly and find their own food when they are just a few days old. They follow their mothers at all times to learn what to eat and where to find the right foods.

Imprinting

A precocial hatchling has a strong **instinct** to stay close to its parents. This instinct, called **imprinting**, is so strong that a baby bird imprints, or memorizes, the first animal it sees. If it hatches without its mother, it may imprint and follow a human, a dog, or another bird.

Help me, Momma!

Unlike precocial babies, **altricial** baby birds are naked and helpless when they hatch. Their eyes are tightly closed. The nestlings stay close together in the nest and wait for their parents to feed them.

These babies must be fed often so that they will grow quickly. When a **nestling** is three days old, it is four times as big as it was when it hatched! After two weeks, it has feathers and can open its eyes.

This hoopoe hovers long enough to feed its hungry nestling and then flies off for more food.

Bright targets

Altricial nestlings have huge brightly colored mouths that make easy targets for parents to "hit" with food. The cardinal, right, puts food directly into its baby's mouth. Most baby birds eat what their parents eat. Some parents **regurgitate**, or bring up, food they have eaten and drop it into the mouths of their babies.

Living up high

Songbirds, crows, herons, raptors, woodpeckers, and pelicans are types of altricial birds. Most altricial birds live high in trees, where their babies are safe from predators during their long stay in the nest. Although precocial birds are more developed when they hatch, altricial babies grow faster and, in the end, develop more quickly.

17

Almost an adult

When a young bird can leave its nest, it is called a fledgling. A fledgling has some of the sturdy feathers it needs to fly, but it still has soft down feathers as well.

During a fledgling's first summer, its down feathers gradually fall out, and mature feathers grow in their place. Shedding and growing feathers is called **molting**.

Less colorful

The fledgling is still immature after its first molt, even though it is nearly the size of its parents. An immature bird is not as colorful as a mature bird. It must finish growing before it develops the coloring of its parents.

(above) This immature king penguin looks half-dressed! Its adult feathers have started to grow in, but the bird has not yet finished molting its down.

Adult colors

Immature birds are dull in color. Dull colors help them hide from predators. Once they are able to escape predators, mature males of some species grow brightly colored feathers.

immature robin

adult male robin

Growing new feathers

Birds continue molting throughout their lives. As they fly, their feathers become damaged. The worn feathers fall out, and new plumage grows in to replace them. Molting keeps feathers ready for flight.

A young yellow-crowned night heron has a gray spotted body, a light face, and short crown feathers.

An adult yellow-crowned night heron has a gray chest, a black and white face, and a yellow crown.

19

Making the long journey

Many birds that enjoy northern climates during the summer cannot survive the long, harsh winters. These birds move to a warmer southern **habitat** for the winter months. Moving between two habitats is called migrating.

Migrating birds fly south in the autumn when the weather starts to change. In the south, the days are longer, the weather is warmer, and there is plenty of food.

Great blue herons that live in northern habitats migrate to Florida, Cuba, and South America. Great blue herons that already live in southern areas stay there all year.

Born to travel

Migration is part of the life cycle of migrating birds, such as the Canada geese above. Their babies hatch in their northern habitats in the spring. By the time fall arrives, the young birds are fully grown and can fly south with the rest of the flock. When spring arrives in the north, the birds fly back there to mate, nest, and lay eggs.

Let's go!

How do migrating birds know exactly when and where to fly? They do not have to be taught. Birds learn by instinct and find their way by watching the sun, stars, coastlines, and landmarks such as mountains.

(above right) Red-winged blackbirds are common migrating birds that live in North America.

Choose me!

In order to make babies, birds mate each spring. Some birds return to the same partner, but others seek out a new mate each year. Female birds usually choose their mating partners. They often sing special songs that tell the males where to find them. Males sing to the females as well, but they also sing to warn other male birds to stay out of their territories.

Male birds perform **courtship displays** to convince females to choose them. Whereas the males of some species have brightly colored feathers year-round, males of other species grow colorful feathers only when it is time to mate. Females see that males with bright feathers are healthy. Female birds look for healthy males as mating partners to ensure that their babies will also be healthy.

Let's dance

Instead of growing bright feathers, some male birds perform courtship dances or fly in dazzling patterns. These athletic displays prove that the males are healthy. Male boobies, on the opposite page, show off their bright blue feet and point their beaks at the sky during courtship. The finches on the right seem to be hugging.

Western grebes dance in fancy patterns on the water and make loud sounds when they are courting.

The male frigate bird has a bright red pouch on his throat that puffs up when he is trying to get the attention of a female frigate bird.

Building a home

After birds choose their mates, they need a safe place to lay their eggs and raise their babies. Some mates work together to find a spot and build their nest. Sometimes only one parent does the work.

Different types of birds build different nests. Most birds build their nests in places that are near food but are hidden from predators.

Safety in numbers
Marine birds often lay eggs and raise their young in a large group called a **nesting colony**. These birds do not need to hide their eggs. There are so many birds in a colony that they are always ready to fight off predators.

Looks good to me!
Some birds, such as these screech owls, do not make their own nests. They move into old nests left by other birds, reptiles, or mammals. Some owls simply lay their eggs and raise their young in hollow trees.

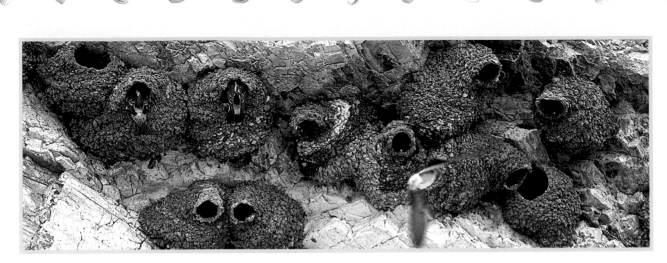

Cliff swallows build mud nests that look like apartments.

Weaverbirds make nests that resemble baskets. The nests hang between stalks of tall marsh grasses.

Built to last

Some large birds, such as ospreys, build their nests out of sticks. These nests are big to begin with, but they get even larger each year. In spring, mating pairs return to the same nest. They add new sticks to fix holes and make the nest stronger.

Disappearing homes

A bird's home includes more than its nest. A nest must be in a habitat with the right food, weather, and shelter. Some birds live in only one type of habitat, such as a seashore, because they eat a certain food or nest in a certain type of tree. Even birds that migrate fly from one specific habitat to another. Many birds cannot adapt to a new habitat.

At least half of all bird species depends on **wetlands**. Wetlands are habitats found between land and water. They include ponds, swamps, marshes, and areas beside rivers, lakes, and oceans. Around the world, birds are threatened by the destruction of wetlands. To survive, they need the food and shelter that only wetlands provide.

Birds such as herons live, feed, and raise their young in wetland areas.

Will I keep my home?

Thousands of species of birds and other animals live in rain forests, but these forests are being destroyed. Rainforest birds cannot live anywhere else. Their nesting trees are found only in this habitat. Once these forests disappear, rainforest birds will have no place to live and will be gone from the earth forever.

Helping birds in danger

People are cutting down trees, clearing the land that birds need to survive, and polluting the environment that all living things share. As a result, many birds are threatened. Some people are taking steps to help birds. Wildlife workers and volunteers help by keeping track of migrating birds, cleaning up waterways, and rescuing birds that are hurt. Many countries have set aside land as **wildlife reserves** for birds. Reserves provide a safe, suitable habitat for birds.

Oil spilled in the ocean coats a bird's feathers and makes it impossible for the bird to fly or swim. The worker above calms an oil-covered bird.

*(above) Bald eagles were **endangered** by the use of pesticides, but people acted quickly to protect them. (inset) This bald eagle was injured, but it was rescued by people who care for birds. After its wing heals, the eagle will leave the Raptor Rehabilitation Center and return to the wild.*

For the birds

You can make your yard a friendly place for birds to rest or build a nest. Follow the tips on these pages, and soon your yard will be filled with feathered friends! You will need the help of an adult to make your yard completely safe for birds.

Try to identify each type of bird you see. Are there different birds in summer than in winter? Watch for families of birds in spring, when eggs hatch and babies grow. Be sure never to touch a nest or eggs, and never disturb the birds!

Use sunflower and thistle seeds in feeders instead of mixed bird seed.

Native plants are plants that grow naturally in your area. When planted in your garden, native plants will attract the insects and small animals that birds need for food.

Add a birdhouse to your yard, and it may become home to a bird family! You can make birdhouses from many household items.

Keep a journal of all the activity you see. Share your observations with your teacher and classmates. Your enthusiasm will inspire others to become bird lovers, too!

Keep your cat indoors when you can so that it cannot chase or injure birds. Even if it wears a bell on its collar, your cat might be able to sneak up on birds.

Birds need a place to drink and bathe. Fill a bird bath or shallow pan with water and make sure you change the water at least twice a week.

Glossary

altricial Describing a baby bird that hatches blind, naked, and helpless

brood To sit on eggs to keep them warm

down A type of soft, fluffy feather

embryo A developing baby animal

endangered Describing an animal species in danger of disappearing

fledgling A young bird that can leave the nest and has some adult feathers

habitat The natural place where a plant or animal is found

hatchling A newly hatched bird

immature Describing an animal that is not yet an adult

instinct A natural awareness or "knowledge" that controls animal behaviors such as migration

mate (v) To join together to make babies; (n) a mating partner

mature Describing a fully grown adult animal

migrate To travel long distances in search of food or better weather

molt To shed and grow new feathers

nestling A baby bird that has not yet left its nest

precocial Describing a baby bird that hatches with feathers and is soon able to see and walk

predator An animal that hunts and eats other animals

species Within a larger group of animals, a smaller group that has the same bodies and habits; for example, bald eagles are a species of birds

wetlands Areas of land next to water that are under shallow water some or all of the time

Index

adults 6, 7, 18, 19
beaks 4, 12, 13, 23
brooding 10-11, 12
dangers 26-27, 28
eggs 7, 8-9, 10, 11, 12-13, 21, 24, 30
embryo 8, 10, 12-13
feathers 4, 13, 14, 16, 18, 19, 22, 23, 28

fledglings 7, 18-19
food 10, 11, 12, 15, 16, 17, 20, 24, 26, 30
habitats 20, 21, 26-27, 28
hatching 6, 7, 8, 11, 13, 14, 15, 16, 17, 21, 30
hatchlings 7, 14-15, 16-17
life cycle 6-7, 21
mating 8, 21, 22-23

migration 7, 20-21, 26
molting 18-19
nests 9, 10, 11, 14, 16, 17, 18, 24-25, 26, 30
nestlings 16-17
parents 8, 10, 11, 12, 15, 16, 17, 18, 24
predators 9, 10, 14, 17, 19, 24

4 5 6 7 8 9 0 Printed in the U.S.A. 1 0 9 8 7 6